DO NOT REMOVE
CARDS FROM POCKET

Everyone Contributes

CLARA HALE

Mother to Those Who Needed One

Bob Italia

Published by Abdo & Daughters, 6535 Cecilia Circle, Edina, Minnesota 55439.

Library bound edition distributed by Rockbottom Books, Pentagon Tower, P.O. Box 36036, Minneapolis, Minnesota 55435.

Edited by Rosemary Wallner

Photo Credits: Wide World - pgs. 10, 13, 16, 20, 23, 28
Bettmann - pgs. 4, 7, 19, 26

Cover Photo: Black Star

Library of Congress Cataloging-in-Publication Data

Italia, Robert, 1955-
      Clara Hale: mother to those who needed one / Bob
Italia; [edited by Rosie Wallner].
                  p.   cm. -- (Everyone Contributes)
      Includes glossary and index.
      Summary: Presents the life of the New York woman whose love of
      children led her to establish a foster care program to help babies born
      addicted to drugs.
      ISBN 1-56239-235-2
      1. Hale, Clara, d. 1992--Juvenile literature. 2. Foster parents--
New York (N.Y.)--Biography--Juvenile literature. 3. Children of narcotic
addicts--New York (N.Y.)--Juvenile literature. 4. Foster home care--New
York (N.Y.)--Juvenile literature. [1. Hale, Clara, d. 1992 2. Foster parents.]
I. Title. II. Series: Italia, Robert, 1955-   Everyone Contributes.
      HQ759.7.I83   1993
      362.7'33'092--dc20
      [B]   93-15261
                                                                          CIP
                                                                          AC

Table of Contents

Clara Hale, noted for her work with drug
addicted infants, shares a happy time with
some children as she celebrates
her 83rd birthday.

Mother Hale

At first glance, the playroom looks like a typical daycare center. Twelve young children rush about the room searching for their coats and sweaters, preparing to go outdoors. A small black woman stands patiently at the door. She smiles as she watches her "children" compete for her attention.

"Watch me, Mommy Hale," a three-year-old boy shouts. "I'm Michael Jackson!"

"Look what I did, Mommy!" says a neatly dressed girl as she proudly holds up a drawing.

All seems well and normal. But these children are anything but normal. They are children of drug addicts. Each was born addicted to drugs.

"Mommy" is Clara Hale. She is the founder of New York's Hale House, a temporary home for child drug addicts. It is the only place of its kind in the United States.

Hospital staffs, police officers, and desperate mothers who have nowhere else to turn bring children to Mother Hale.

The children range in age from two weeks to three years. Most stay at Hale House for about 18 months. Then they are either placed in foster homes or returned to their natural mothers.

Hale's mission is to nurture these children from the pain of their inherited addiction. She helps them to begin a happy, healthy, and prosperous life.

A Foundation of Love

Clara Hale was born and raised in Philadelphia, Pennsylvania, the youngest of four children. Her father died when she was a baby. Her mother supported the family by cooking and renting out part of their house to boarders. "My mother taught me to love people," Hale said. "She gave me the foundation for all I've done."

After graduating from high school, Hale married Thomas Hale and moved to New York. There, her husband began a floorwaxing business. "He didn't make enough money," Hale recalled. "So I did domestic work at night, cleaning theaters."

Clara Hale's five-room apartment becomes a foster home for many children.

By the time she was 27 years old, Hale had two children, Lorraine and Nathan. But then her husband died of cancer—leaving Hale without any financial support.

"I didn't want my children left alone," Hale said, "so I began caring for other people's children during the day. The parents paid me. I didn't make a whole lot, but I wasn't starving. And the kids must have liked it, because once they got there, they didn't want to go home. So what started as day-care ended up being full time. The parents would see the children on weekends."

Clara Hale suddenly found that she was a foster parent. People who had problems in their family let their children stay with Hale for a while. For the next 30 years, Hale's five-room apartment on 146th Street became home for seven to eight foster children at a time.

"My daughter says she was almost 16 before she realized all these other kids weren't her real sisters and brothers," said Hale. "Everyone called me 'Mommy.' I took care of 40 of them like that. They're now all grown up. They're doctors, lawyers, everything. Almost all of them stay in touch. I have about 60 grandchildren."

By then, Hale was ready to retire as a foster parent. "When I was 65," she recalled, "I decided to give up taking care of children. Prices were getting very high, and I thought I'd had enough." Caring for baby drug addicts was never on her mind.

"But one day," she continued, "my daughter saw this woman on the street with a baby in her arms. She was an addict and she kept nodding off, almost dropping the baby. My daughter went over, asked if she needed help and told her about me. The next day, the girl arrived at my door with the baby. We decided to take the baby in. She was only two months old. The mother told her friends, and inside of two months, we were taking care of 22 children."

When a woman is pregnant, everything she eats or drinks affects the baby. If a pregnant woman takes drugs, the drugs flow from the mother's bloodstream into her baby's bloodstream. As a result, the unborn baby becomes addicted to the same drug the mother is addicted to. When the baby is born, he or she shows all the signs of a drug addict.

Dr. Lorraine Hale, president of Hale House and daughter of Clara Hale, kisses the hand of four-year-old Paul while his mother watches.

"When they first came to me," she continued, "I had never seen any child addicts before. They scratch themselves and keep nodding off, just like grown-up addicts. They make all kinds of faces. They're pitiful to see. I knew that if we fed them drugs, they would grow up to be drug addicts. Whatever we could do to get them off, we had to do while they were young. I just give them love and plenty of food. I sing to them. Walk the floor with them. And in a month's time, it's all over.

"I love children," Hale added. "I think all children are born with something special. And you can bring it out and make them good people. But they need the right start. They need love."

Hale received financial support from her own children, who had successful careers. Lorraine had a Ph.D. in child development. Nathan was a Certified Public Accountant (C.P.A.), and Kenneth, her adopted son, was a doctor of education. With their help, Hale cared for addicted babies in her apartment for a year and a half.

"The city first heard about me when someone told them there was a crazy lady taking in people's children and not charging them," Hale explained. "They were addicts. They didn't have anything to give. Then someone suggested we write to the city.

They gave us money right away. They also helped us find a larger place." Hale needed the room—lots of it.

Hale House

The city found a five-story brownstone for Hale on West 122nd Street in the Harlem section of New York City. The building, which used to be a rooming house, was completely gutted and remodeled. Hale moved into her new home in 1975. She called it Hale House.

On the first floor, she filled the playroom with books and toys. Next to the playroom was a kitchen, well-stocked with food obtained from a wholesaler.

The second floor contained the nursery. Hale decorated the room with bright floral wallpaper. She put nine cribs in the nursery for the addicted babies. Clara Hale lived on the third floor of Hale House. She decorated her room with lace curtains and Victorian lamps. Her room also had a rocking chair. She rocked and comforted the addicted babies through their pain.

Clara Hale holds an infant she is caring for in
her second-floor nursery.

"When there's a newborn baby," Hale said, "I put the crib in here with me. I keep it here for four months. Usually, by then, there's no sign of drugs anymore, and they can sleep through the night."

Next to Hale's bedroom, there was a living room. It had comfortable blue-and-white couches, thick blue rugs, and a baby grand piano. The room served a special purpose—to help heal old wounds.

"The children come up here when their mothers visit," Hale said. "I want them to have a nice place they can feel good about. The families see how their children have lived here, and they really try to do the same. These are generally nice people. They've made a mistake. We're all entitled to a mistake."

The parents who brought their children to Hale House were drug abusers. One such parent was Nancy, whose son, Raphael, stayed at Hale House. Nancy was on drugs for five years. She supported her habit by selling drugs and robbing people. But then the law caught up to her. Nancy was arrested and put into prison for four years.

When Nancy got out of prison, she started using drugs again. That's when she became pregnant with Raphael. The father of Nancy's baby was also a drug addict. Nancy didn't think that her baby would have a drug problem.

But when he was born, Raphael had bouts with tremors. Eventually, Nancy brought Raphael to Hale House.

Most parents let their children stay at Hale House while they get help for their addiction. Once they begin to recover, they return for their children. Some parents did not return, however. So Hale put their children up for adoption.

The purpose of Hale House was to reunite the children with their parents. Adoption was the final option. By 1984, more than 500 children had come under Mother Hale's care. Only twelve had been put up for adoption. And by 1990, Hale and her staff had cared for over 800 babies.

Hale was fiercely protective of her children even when adoptive parents were found. She sometimes turned down prospective parents if they did not make a good impression. "We arrange [the adoption] through the Children's Aid Society," Hale stated. "But they have to bring the parents here, and I have to OK them. They don't just take my children anyplace."

Dr. Lorraine Hale was the director of Hale House. She took care of the business details so her mother could concentrate on the children. In 1984, Hale House operated on $147,000. Of that total, the city provided $122,000.

Many famous people supported Hale House.
Filmmaker Spike Lee contributed
$100,000 to support Clara Hale's campaign
to save addicted babies.

The rest was donated. One famous supporter was former Beatle John Lennon. He donated money to keep Hale House open. Still, there never seemed to be enough money.

"We are poor continually," Lorraine Hale said. "All the staff is terribly underpaid—an average of $175 a week. They stay because they are devoted."

The city allowed Hale House to take care of only 15 children at a time. There was always a waiting list. Often, 30 or more children waited for an opening.

While Hale cared for the children, their parents went through a drug-treatment program that lasted about 18 months. "There aren't that many good drug programs," Lorraine Hale said. "But we're happy with ours. We have never had a case where the mother went back on drugs."

The program worked for the children as well. The oldest children who had come to Hale House as baby addicts did not become involved with drugs. But the news wasn't all good. These same children did not do well in school. The addiction passed on to them from their mothers affected their ability to learn.

Hale and her staff never told the children that they were born addicted to drugs. They thought that this dreadful news would give the children a poor image of themselves.

Though Clara Hale became emotionally attached to her children, she was never sad to see them go. "What keeps me from being unhappy is that when one leaves, it always seems they bring me in a baby," she said. "I don't have time to worry about the one who's left. Also, you've got to tell yourself from the very beginning that this is not your child. God was good to me. He gave me a son and a daughter. So I have nothing to worry about. And since then, I've had children and children and children."

Hale gave much of her time to her children. But she never complained. "I have nothing but love to give them," she stated. "Giving it makes me happy. And when they come back later on, and I've seen that they turned out well, I feel really good. It's been a lovely life. Believe me, I have no regrets."

Throughout the years, Hale worked hard to care for her children. Slowly, she gained recognition for her outstanding efforts. In 1985, President Ronald Reagan singled her out as a true American hero.

President Ronald Reagan meets with Clara Hale. Reagan singled out Hale "as a true American hero."

Clara Hale worked hard for city and federal support for Hale House. Here she holds a check for $1.1 million in federal funds.
With her is Senator Alfonse D'Amato, her daughter Lorraine, and New York Representative Charles Rangel.

By 1989, Hale House received $370,000 a year from the city and state. Another $400,000 was donated. Then Hale received more national attention for her work. In March 1989, she was named the winner of the Truman Award for Public Service.

Homeward Bound

That same year, Hale began a new program called Hale House Homeward Bound. Homeward Bound was a new $2 million housing development with nearly 35 apartments. The program was for young women who had completed treatment in drug rehabilitation centers and were trying to turn their lives around.

In January 1990, Hale House Homeward Bound received the help of a famous volunteer. Leona Helmsley, the owner of the Helmsley Palace hotel in New York City, had been convicted of cheating on her taxes. As part of her sentence, she agreed to spend 750 hours of community service time at the project.

Hale welcomed Helmsley's help. She felt it was a wonderful idea to have a woman of Helmsley's stature working with needy women.

She also felt that Helmsley could teach the women about the hotel business and help them get jobs.

"Amen"

On February 12, 1990, Hale made a special guest appearance on the NBC-TV show "Amen." In an episode called "The Talent Show," Reverend Gregory, played by Clifton Davis, welcomed Mother Hale on stage during the church's annual charity revue. Gregory sang "You're My Child" while a film about Hale House was shown. After the song, Gregory declared that the proceeds of the talent show would be donated to Hale House.

Hale's appearance on the show was the idea of Executive producer Ed Weinberger and series star Anna Maria Horsford. Horsford had told Weinberger about Clara Hale's wonderful work in Harlem. Weinberger was impressed. He decided to make a donation to Hale House and invited Clara Hale to appear on the show. Hale's appearance brought much-needed attention to her work.

Many famous and important people have supported
Clara Hale. Here she poses with
former U.S. Surgeon General C. Everett Koop (left)
and Senator Alfonse D'Amato.

A Future in Doubt

Hale House's future never seemed brighter. But in 1990, a dark cloud suddenly drifted over Hale House, casting a shadow of doubt. City Hall decided to shut down Hale House. Welfare officials said that enough foster homes had been found for babies of drug addicts. Agency-run nurseries, like Hale House, were no longer needed. The city also felt that foster homes were the best places to raise young children. Many child-care experts agreed.

But Clara Hale had other thoughts. "I am not going to give it up," she said. "These are God's children and he intends them to be here and for me to take care of them." Hale refused to believe that her work was not needed or had no value.

The city stopped referring infants to Hale House. Ten children remained in Hale's care, waiting to be returned to their parents or relatives. With the future in doubt, Hale turned to her supporters.

Hale House began an emergency direct-mail fund-raising effort. They also printed 100,000 bumper stickers that read: "The city says no. We say yes. Support Hale House." Almost immediately, private donations poured in.

While Hale battled City Hall, the National Coalition of 100 Black Women (NCBW) honored her. The group gave Hale the Candace (pronounced Can-DAY-say) Award. The award is named after the ancient Ethiopian title for empress. Each year, it is given to 10 outstanding black Americans. The award honors people with strong character and great personal results in their fields.

Scared Straight

Hale kept busy with her children. She also took time to speak to a group of 14-year-old boys and girls. The children were all awaiting trials on drug-related charges.

The Department of Juvenile Justice arranged the meeting. The department hoped that the young inmates might benefit from seeing where drugs ultimately lead—into the tiny brains and bodies of innocent babies.

As she talked to the young people, Hale was direct but encouraging. She hoped to make them feel good about themselves. Then perhaps she could help them overcome the cycle of drugs and crime and hopelessness.

At President Reagan's State of the Union address, Clara Hale is applauded for her hard work and efforts. On her right is First Lady Nancy Reagan.

"Just be proud you're black," Hale told the group. "We're a great people." Then she encouraged the group to get along with everybody. "Don't hate," she said.

By April 1991, Hale House had received tens of thousands of dollars in contributions from people around the country. A group of 250 city churches also provided funds. Clara Hale was thrilled.

"God has given me the responsibility to care for these children," she said. "And now we are going to be able to provide for them even better than before."

Hale House was back in business. By 1992, Hale and her staff had nurtured more than 1,000 drug-addicted babies.

In November, Clara Hale suffered a minor stroke. She was recovering when suddenly, on December 18, 1992, she died of complications from the stroke. She was 87 years old.

Clara "Mother" Hale, founder of the Hale
House, holds a young boy on her lap in New
York during the announcement of the establishment
of the nation's first full-time residential home
for care of infants infected with AIDS.

Clara Hale's Legacy

With Hale's death, the world lost an extraordinarily caring and loving human being. But her nurturing and healing ways live on in the house that still bears her name. The success of Hale House has shown the world that love and understanding can overcome the most serious problems—even drug addiction. Even more, Hale House has provided a way to restore hope and happiness to those whose lives seem hopeless and destined for ruin.

As Nancy, a mother and recovering addict, said: "Mother Hale is about the best thing that happened to me in my whole life. She's given me and Raphael a chance to make it."

We all have Clara Hale to thank for showing us the way.

GLOSSARY

Addict—A person who has let himself or herself be taken over by a drug or habit.

Adopt—To take legally into one's own family and raise as one's own child.

Brownstone—A reddish-brown sandstone used for building.

Coalition—A combination or union.

Drug—Any substance used as or in a medicine; a narcotic.

Foster children—Children who are raised in someone else's home.

Foster home—A home where children from another family are raised.

Foster parents—Parents who raise other people's children.

Heredity—The transmission from parent to child of certain characteristics.

Inherited—To receive certain characteristics by heredity.

Narcotic—A drug that induces sleep and relief of pain.

Stroke—A sudden paralysis caused by the breaking or obstruction of a blood vessel in the brain.

Tremors—A trembling, shaking feeling.

Welfare officer—A person who manages the money or other aid the government gives to people in need.

Wholesaler—A person who sells goods in large quantities.

INDEX